THE
CHARCOAL COMPANION®
STUFFED
BURGER
✦ RECIPE BOOK ✦

©2012 The Companion Group

Berkeley, California

800-521-0505

www.companion-group.com

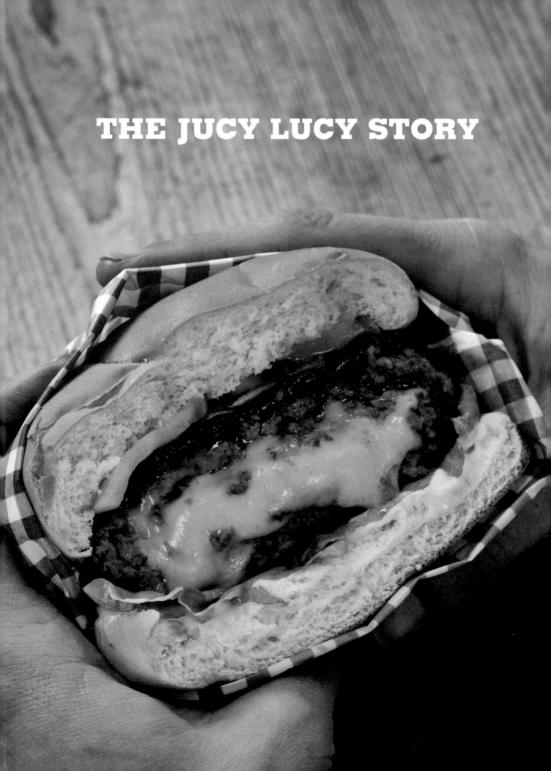

THE JUCY LUCY STORY

The origins of the Jucy Lucy are shrouded in mystery. Was it born within the wood-paneled walls of Matt's Bar, a working-class dive at 3500 Cedar Avenue, in South Minneapolis? Or did it come into being in the 5-8 Club, a former speakeasy just a few blocks down the same street?

It was an inventive customer, says Cheryl Bristol, direct descendent of the original "Matt" of "Matt's Bar." Back then, the bar was called "Mr. Nibbs" and Matt Bristol was just a bartender with a dream of one day buying the joint he tended bar in. "The whole story goes like this:" she told a reporter from Minneapolis City Pages in 1998. "There was a bachelor customer who used to come in every day and order a burger. One day, in 1954, he told the cook to seal up some cheese in the middle. So the cook did, and when he bit into it the hot cheese spurted out, and he wiped his mouth and said, 'Oooh, that's one Juicy lucy!' They used to talk goofy like that back then."

"He started making them at his customers request," added Scott Nelson, in an interview with another reporter hot on the trail of the Jucy Lucy's origins - this time from the *Minneapolis Daily*. Nelson bought the bar from Bristol in 1998. "He hated making them. They were a pain in the butt." Still, Bristol was aware that the bar's clientele really enjoyed eating them. When "Mr. Nibbs" became "Matt's Bar," Bristol commissioned a bar menu with the hit sandwich on it. It came back with a typo - "Jucy Lucy," Bristol, a pragmatic man, declared it close enough. Balderdash. "Ours is truly a juicy burger," 5-8 Club marketing director Jill Scogenheim told the Daily. "We spell it the way it's meant to be spelled."

"If it's spelled correctly," says Nelson. "You're in the wrong place."

Cheeseburger pilgrims will find both establishments still doing a brisk business. Matt's serves them no frills, served up on a single sheet of greasy waxed paper. Nelson sticks to the blueprint set down by the original customer - a burger that envelops a single slice of American cheese (No more, says Nelson, since the goal is to have the cheese completely liquified), grilled until the edges are charred, liberally seasoned with salt and pepper. Holding to tradition hasn't hurt business any - a showdown between Matt's and the 5-8 hosted by the television show Food Wars resulted in Matt's walking away with the title of Best Lucy.

The 5-8 Club plays a little more fast and loose with their recipe - stuffing their burgers with whatever strikes their fancy. They hold an annual Lucy-eating contest and give out a Charlie and the Chocolate Factory-inspired "Golden Lucy" that entitles the holder to a year of endless burgers. Still other Minneapolis bars serve further variations on the Lucy - burgers stuffed with blue cheese and garlic, jalapeño and jack cheese, or a Frankenstein-inspired burger called the Mary Shelley, which is bisected by a slice of bacon, so that it's ends stick out of either side like the bolts of Frankenstein's neck. Minnesota's long cold winters have proven a lively incubator for new kinds of molten cheese technology.

Which is to say - take these recipes as a guide, sure, but also use them as a jumping-off point for your own adventures. For such a simple concept, there's a lot of room for creativity.

And now, as you set off on your own experimental Jucy Lucy adventures, remember one thing: Wait. Seriously. Contemplate the burger that you are about to eat. Otherwise, the cheese will be so molten that it will napalm your taste buds.

And with that...Enjoy.

THE CHARCOAL COMPANION
STUFFED BURGER RECIPE BOOK

HOW TO STUFF-A-BURGER:

All the burger recipes in this book yield 4 juicy, delicious three-quarter pound burgers. We recommend using the Charcoal Companion® Stuff-A-Burger™ Press and Basket for best results.

STEP 1: Place ½ lb. ground meat into the press and use the small side of the lid to form a well for toppings.

STEP 2: Fill center with desired toppings.

STEP 3: Place ¼ lb. ground meat on top. You may use the inside of the lid to form the top layer.

STEP 4: Use the flat side of the lid to seal burger.

V

ALL-AMERICAN

The classic burger that started it all... but with a slight innovation! In our All-American, the dill and onion are inside the burger as well as riding up on top. Those interested in following the Matt's Bar formula should remember to use a single slice of American cheese and lots of salt and pepper while grilling. The more 5-8 Club-inclined should add more cheese and go easy on the seasoning.

Ingredients:

3 lbs.	ground beef	¼ c.	white onion, chopped
1 tbsp.	ketchup	¼ c.	dill pickle, chopped
1 tbsp.	mustard	4	hamburger buns
8 oz.	cheddar cheese, grated		

Method:

Combine ground beef, mustard, and ketchup in a mixing bowl, using hands to mix thoroughly. To form burgers, place ½ pound of ground beef mixture into the bottom of the burger press. Push the long end of the press into the meat to form a well. Stuff the burger with 2 ounces of cheddar cheese and 1 tsp. each chopped white onion and dill pickle. Place ¼ pound of ground beef mixture on top of the stuffing, and use the press to seal. Repeat process for other three burgers. Cook over direct heat until thoroughly cooked. Serve burger on bun garnished with more sliced onions, pickles, mustard, and ketchup.

Yield: 4 stuffed burgers

WHERE THE BUFFALO CHICKEN ROAM

New York, New York is a wonderful town, but when it comes to mouth-watering chicken wings, Buffalo has got it down! This burger is just like one of their delicious battered and sauced chicken wings, but in stuffed and juicy form.

Ingredients:

3 lbs.	ground chicken	1 c.	shredded iceberg lettuce
½ c.	bread crumbs		
2 tbsp.	hot sauce	½ c.	ranch style salad dressing
½ c.	chopped celery		
8 oz.	bleu cheese crumbles	4	ciabatta style hamburger buns

Method:

Combine ground chicken, bread crumbs, hot sauc , salt, and pepper to taste in mixing bowl, using hands to mix thoroughly. To form burgers, place ½ pound of ground chicken mixture into the bottom of the burger press. Push the long end of the press into the meat to form a well. Stuff the burger with 2 tbsp. celery and 2 ounces bleu cheese crumbles. Place ¼ pound of chicken mixture on top of the stuffing and use the press to seal. Repeat process for other three burgers. Cook over direct heat until thoroughly cooked. Serve burger on bun garnished with ranch-style dressing, iceberg lettuce, and additional bleu cheese and hot sauce, if desired.

Yield: 4 stuffed burgers

THE EL PASO

The El Paso represents the many border towns where America and Mexico meet and make beautiful food together. If you want more cross-border adventures, substitute cotjia cheese for pepper jack, pico de gallo for the black beans and sour cream, and add as many jalapeño or serrano chiles as you can stand!

Ingredients:

3 lbs.	ground beef	1/3 c.	pico de gallo
2 tbsp.	taco seasoning	1 c.	romaine lettuce, shredded
8 oz.	pepper jack cheese, grated	2 tbsp.	fresh cilantro, chopped
½ c.	black beans, drained	4	crusty hamburger buns
½ c.	sour cream		

Method:

Combine ground beef and taco seasoning in a mixing bowl, using hands to mix thoroughly. To form burgers, place ½ pound of ground beef mixture into the bottom of the burger press. Push the long end of the press into the meat to form a well. Stuff the burger with 2 ounces of pepper jack cheese and 1 tbsp. black beans. Place ¼ pound of ground beef mixture on top of the stuffing and use the press to seal. Repeat process for other three burgers. Cook over direct heat until thoroughly cooked. In a small bowl, combine sour cream and pico de gallo. Serve cooked burger on a bun garnished with sour cream mixture, romaine, and chopped cilantro.

Yield: 4 stuffed burgers

BANH MI

This great Vietnamese sandwich is actually a mixture of Vietnamese and French food influences. We're adding a third: American barbecue. The result is more substantial than a traditional Banh Mi, but just as delicious.

Ingredients:

½ c.	carrot, grated	3 lbs.	ground pork
½ c.	daikon, grated	1 tbsp.	fish sauce
½ c.	cucumber, chopped	½ tbsp.	fresh garlic, chopped
½ c.	jalapeno, chopped	¼ c.	mayonnaise
1 tbsp.	rice vinegar	4	baguette-style buns
1/3 c.	fresh cilantro, chopped		

Method:

Make a slaw by combining carrot, daikon, cucumber, jalapeno, rice vinegar, and cilantro in a small bowl. Set aside.

Combine ground pork, fish sauce, and garlic in mixing bowl, using hands to mix thoroughly. To form burgers, place ½ pound of pork mixture into the bottom of the burger press. Push the long end of the press into the meat to form a well. Stuff the burger with ¼ cup of the slaw prepared earlier. Place ¼ pound of ground pork mixture on top of the stuffing and use the press to seal. Repeat process for other three burgers. Cook over direct heat until thoroughly cooked. Serve burger on bun garnished with mayonnaise, more slaw, and fresh cilantro.

Yield: 4 stuffed burgers

THE COWBOY

This burger rides tall in the saddle, and is packed with everything a cowboy needs to fulfill his duties out on the range. Head to the chuck wagon and get grubbin' on this burger with onion rings, barbecue sauce, and bacon, plus enough beef to make the cattle herd nervous.

Ingredients:

1	medium yellow onion, chopped	8 oz.	cheddar cheese, grated
1 tbsp.	olive oil	6	strips of bacon, cooked
3 lbs.	ground beef	8	onion rings, cooked
2 tbsp.	barbecue sauce	4	hamburger buns

Method:

Heat a small sauté pan and add olive oil. Add chopped onions and cook over medium heat, stirring occasionally, until thoroughly browned. Season with salt and pepper to taste and set aside to cool. Crumble two strips of bacon and set aside.

Combine ground beef and barbecue sauce in a mixing bowl, using hands to mix thoroughly. To form burgers, place ½ pound of ground beef mixture into the bottom of the burger press. Push the long end of the press into the meat to form a well. Stuff the burger with 2 ounces of cheddar cheese, 1 tbsp. crumbled bacon, and 2 tsp. caramelized onions. Place ¼ pound of ground beef mixture on top of the stuffing and use the press to seal. Repeat process for other three burgers. Cook over direct heat until thoroughly cooked. Serve burger on bun garnished with more barbecue sauce, 1 slice of bacon, and 2 onion rings. Try not to die.

Yield: 4 stuffed burgers

DON'T GO BREAKING YOUR HEART

This lighter version of the Lucy is still just as juicy! The main components are there: meat stuffed with cheese, but by replacing them with heart-healthy alternatives, you get a sandwich that's a delicious, low-cholesterol option.

Ingredients:

3 lbs.	ground chicken breast	8 oz.	cottage cheese, drained
1 tsp.	lemon zest, finely chopped	1	avocado
1 tsp.	fresh rosemary, finely chopped	1	large tomato, sliced
		4	whole wheat hamburger buns

Method:

Drain the cottage cheese and set aside.

Combine ground chicken breast, lemon zest, fresh rosemary, salt, and pepper to taste in mixing bowl, using hands to mix thoroughly. To form burgers, place ½ pound of chicken breast mixture into the bottom of the burger press. Push the long end of the press into the meat to form a well. Stuff the burger with 2 ounces of drained cottage cheese. Place ¼ pound of chicken mixture on top of the stuffing and use the press to seal. Repeat process for other three burgers. Cook over direct heat until thoroughly cooked. Serve burger on bun garnished with Dijon mustard, sliced avocado, and tomato.

Yield: 4 stuffed burgers

IN THE GARDEN OF BURGER

A vegan Lucy? Yes, it can be done! This vegan version stuffs your burger with avocado and red onion, resulting in a moist sandwich with a little bit of crunch. For a more Middle Eastern variation, use falafel mix instead and substitute hummus for the avocado.

Ingredients:

2	boxes dry veggie burger mix (10 oz. each)	½ c.	green goddess salad dressing
1	large avocado	4	lettuce leaves
¼ c.	fresh lemon juice	8	slices ripe tomato
½ c.	chopped red onion	4	whole wheat, crusty hamburger buns

Method:

Prepare the veggie burger mix according to package instructions. Set aside. Meanwhile, peel and seed the avocado. Mash with lemon juice and season to taste with salt and pepper. Set aside until ready to use.

To form the burgers, line the burger press with plastic wrap, allowing some to drape over the edges of the press. Place ¾ cup of burger mix into the bottom of the press and push the long end of the press into the mixture to form a well. Stuff the burger with 2 tbsp. avocado mash and 2 tbsp. chopped red onion. Add another ¼ cup of veggie burger mixture on top of the stuffing and fold the plastic wrap over the top. Place the top on the press and push down to seal. Remove the burger from the press and remove the plastic wrap. Repeat process for the remaining three burgers. Pan fry over medium heat in a nonstick pan until browned on both sides. Serve burger on bun garnished with green goddess dressing, lettuce leaves, and ripe tomato slices.

Yield: 4 stuffed burgers

THE GOBBLE GOBBLER

Some would say that the fourth Thursday of November turkey dinner is a sacred feast, meant only to be consumed on Thanksgiving Day. Others would argue that if something is so good, why wait 364 days to enjoy the flavors of this most special of American eating holidays? Serve up the Gobble Gobbler at your next family gathering and get all the deliciousness of Turkey Day without having to listen to Aunt Edna's cat stories over and over.

Ingredients:

3 lbs.	ground turkey		1 c.	mashed potatoes
1 tsp.	dried sage		¼ c.	gravy
¼ c.	prepared turkey stuffing		4	Kaiser hamburger buns
2 tbsp.	cranberry sauce			

Method:

Combine ground turkey, dried sage, salt, and pepper to taste in a mixing bowl, using hands to mix thoroughly. To form burgers, place ½ pound of turkey mixture into the bottom of the burger press. Push the long end of the press into the meat to form a well. Stuff the burger with 1 tbsp. of turkey stuffing and ½ tbsp. of cranberry sauce. Place ¼ pound of ground turkey mixture on top of the stuffing and use the press to seal. Repeat process for other three burgers. Cook over direct heat until thoroughly cooked. Serve burger on toasted bun garnished with warm mashed potatoes, gravy, and more cranberry sauce.

Yield: 4 stuffed burgers

BLT BURGER

The BLT is a classic sandwich, but it has the tendency to be a bit on the dry side. Problem solved! Take a few key ingredients and use them as filling instead to keep your lunch nice and moist. Your comfort food suddenly got a lot more comfortable.

Ingredients:

1 c.	chopped tomatoes	¼ c.	mayonnaise
3 lbs.	ground beef	4	crisp lettuce leaves
8 oz.	fontina cheese, grated	4	toasted hamburger buns
½ c.	cooked and crumbled bacon		

Method:

Prepare a small tomato salad by placing chopped tomatoes into a bowl and sprinkling them with salt and pepper to taste. Set aside.

Combine ground beef with salt and pepper to taste in a mixing bowl, using hands to mix thoroughly. To form burgers, place ½ pound of ground beef mixture into the bottom of the burger press. Push the long end of the press into the meat to form a well. Stuff the burger with 2 ounces of grated fontina and 2 tbsp. crumbled bacon. Place ¼ lb. of the ground beef mixture on top of the stuffing and use the press to seal. Repeat process for other three burgers. Cook over direct heat until thoroughly cooked. Serve burger on a toasted hamburger bun garnished with mayonnaise, lettuce, tomato salad, and more bacon, if desired.

Yield: 4 stuffed burgers

THE CORDON BLEU

Did you know that the Cordon Bleu is an American – not French – invention? It is, and it also makes for an amazing burger experience. You can change things up by mixing your bread crumbs with egg and using them to batter the outside of the burger instead of mixing them in, resulting in an even crisper patty.

Ingredients:

3 lbs.	ground chicken	1 c.	Swiss cheese, grated
¾ c.	seasoned bread crumbs	¼ c.	Dijon mustard
1 tsp.	fresh thyme, minced	1	large baguette, cut into 4 pieces
2 c.	ham, chopped		

Method:

Combine ground chicken, bread crumbs, fresh thyme, salt and pepper to taste in mixing bowl, using hands to mix thoroughly. To form burgers, place ½ pound of ground chicken mixture into the bottom of the burger press. Push the long end of the press into the meat to form a well. Stuff the burger with ½ cup ham and ¼ cup Swiss cheese. Place ¼ pound of chicken mixture on top of the stuffing and use the press to seal. Repeat process for other three burgers. Heat a large sauté pan over medium heat. Add 1 tbsp. oil and pan fry burgers until golden brown on all sides. Serve burger with baguette, Dijon Mustard and green salad dressed with your favorite vinaigrette.

Yield: 4 stuffed burgers

THE JERK

Spicy and sweet, Caribbean-style. Take a bite and close your eyes, and you're transported to a warm, sandy beach – even if you're just in your own kitchen. This pork burger combines sweet, juicy pineapple with jalapeños for a truly exotic island experience.

Ingredients:

4	pineapple rings, grilled	1 c.	sour cream
4	jalapeño peppers, grilled	2 tbsp.	fresh lime juice (divided)
1	shallot, chopped	3 lbs.	ground pork
1	garlic clove, chopped	2 tbsp.	jerk seasoning
1 c.	fresh cilantro, stemmed and chopped	½ c.	chopped green onions
		4	crusty hamburger buns

Method:

Heat grill or grill pan to medium-high. Grill pineapple rings and jalapeño peppers until they begin to char. Chop pineapple into large chunks and set aside. Remove the stem and seeds of the jalapeños, chop roughly, and set aside.

Make a dressing by adding the shallot, garlic, cilantro, sour cream, and 1 tbsp. of fresh lime juice to a blender or food processor. Combine until smooth. Transfer to a container and refrigerate until ready for use.

Combine ground pork, jerk seasoning, and remaining lime juice in mixing bowl, using hands to mix thoroughly. To form burgers, place ½ pound of ground pork mixture into the bottom of the burger press. Push the long end of the press into the meat to form a well. Stuff the burger with 2 tbsp. chopped grilled pineapple, 1 tbsp. jalapeño, and 1 tbsp. chopped green onion. Place ¼ pound of pork mixture on top of the stuffing and use the press to seal. Repeat process for other three burgers. Cook over direct heat until thoroughly cooked. Serve burger on bun garnished with sour cream dressing.

Yield: 4 stuffed burgers

THE GREAT WALL

Forget calling for take-out: this Asian-influenced burger will satisfy your cravings better than any limp chow mein. The Great Wall features cabbage, bean sprouts, soy sauce, and peanuts, making it a delicious meal to enjoy before a kung fu movie marathon.

Ingredients:

1 tbsp.	peanut oil	2 tbsp.	soy sauce
2 c.	Chinese cabbage, thinly sliced (aka Napa)	3 lbs.	ground pork
		2	cloves garlic, minced
½ c.	fresh carrots, julienned	2 tsp.	spicy mustard
¼ c.	red onion, thinly sliced	2 tbsp.	fresh parsley, chopped
½ c.	bean sprouts	4	large lettuce leaves

Method:

Heat a large sauté pan. Add the peanut oil and sauté cabbage, carrots, onion, and bean sprouts until slightly wilted, about 4-5 minutes. Add soy sauce and cook another 1-2 minutes until most of the liquid has disappeared. Set aside.

Combine ground pork, garlic, spicy mustard, fresh parsley, salt, and pepper to taste in mixing bowl, using hands to mix thoroughly. To form burgers, place ½ pound of ground pork mixture into the bottom of the burger press. Push the long end of the press into the meat to form a well. Stuff the burger with ¼ cup of the cooked cabbage mixture. Place ¼ pound of pork mixture on top of the stuffing and use the press to seal. Repeat process for other three burgers. Cook over direct heat until thoroughly cooked. Serve burger on a lettuce leaf garnished with more of the cabbage mixture, soy sauce, and chopped peanuts, if desired.

Yield: 4 stuffed burgers

THE SALSICCIA

Italian sausage, mozzarella, and marinara make for a hearty, homespun Italian burger. This is the perfect sandwich to toss back after a day spent hiking the Tuscan countryside... or just cleaning out your garage.

Ingredients:

1 tbsp.	olive oil	8 oz.	mozzarella cheese, grated
½ c.	crimini mushrooms, sliced	⅓ c.	marinara sauce
½ tbsp.	minced garlic	½ c.	ricotta
1 ½ lbs.	mild Italian sausage, bulk or casings removed	2 tbsp.	fresh basil, chopped
1 ½ lbs	ground beef	4	foccacia-style buns, slightly toasted
1 tbsp.	pesto		

Method:

Heat a small skillet over medium heat and add olive oil. Add garlic to pan and sauté until fragrant, about one minute. Add mushrooms and sauté until golden brown, about 4 minutes. Remove from heat and set aside.

Combine sausage, beef, and pesto in a mixing bowl, using hands to mix thoroughly. To form burgers, place ½ pound of meat mixture into the bottom of the burger press. Push the long end of the press into the meat to form a well. Stuff the burger with 2 ounces of mozzarella cheese and 1 tbsp. sautéed mushrooms. Place another ¼ pound of meat mixture on top of the stuffing and use the press to seal. Repeat process for other three burgers. Cook over direct heat until thoroughly cooked. Serve burgers on lightly toasted foccacia style buns, garnished with marinara sauce, ricotta, and a sprinkle of chopped basil.

Yield: 4 stuffed burgers

AUSSIE ON THE BARBIE

You call that a burger? THIS is a burger! For real, mate – this is what they do down under: dress a burger with grilled pineapple rings, pickled beets, and chile mayonnaise. If you've been a good sheila or bloke, they'll add a fried egg on top. Here, we present the stuffed version.

Ingredients:

3 lbs.	ground beef	2 tbsp.	mayonnaise
6	pineapple rings	1 tbsp.	Sirracha hot sauce or other hot chile sauce
12	pickled beets, sliced		
8 oz.	Gouda cheese, shredded	1 tbsp.	fresh chopped parsley
4	eggs	4	crusty hamburger rolls

Method:

Preheat your grill or grill pan to medium-high. Grill pineapple rings until they begin to lightly char and soften. When cool enough to handle, chop two rings into small chunks and set aside with the other grilled pineapple rings.

Drain and pat dry the pickled beets. Chop four slices into small chunks and set aside with the remaining beet slices.

Make a chile mayonnaise by combining mayonnaise and one tsp. of Sirracha in a small bowl. Set aide.

Combine ground beef, 2 tsp. Sirracha, salt, and pepper to taste in mixing bowl, using hands to mix thoroughly. To form burgers, place ½ pound of ground beef mixture into the bottom of the burger press. Push the long end of the press into the meat to form a well. Stuff the burger with 2 ounces of Gouda cheese, 1 tsp. grilled pineapple chunks, and 1 tsp. chopped pickled beets. Place ¼ pound of beef mixture on top of the stuffing and use the press to seal. Repeat process for other three burgers. Cook over direct heat until thoroughly cooked. Meanwhile, prepare four fried eggs in a skillet and keep warm. Serve burger on a toasted bun garnished with chile mayonnaise, more sliced pickled beets, grilled pineapple rings, a fried egg, and chopped parsley.

Yield: 4 stuffed burgers

BEEFY DIONYSUS

This beefy lamb burger is a big, savory mess – a juicy tribute to the god of good wine, good food, and getting down. With decadent melted feta and a hint of red wine, this Olympian burger is a fitting offering to the gods... and your friends!

Ingredients:

1½ lbs.	ground beef		8 oz.	feta cheese, crumbled
1½ lbs.	ground lamb		¼ c.	red onion, chopped
2 tbsp.	red wine		¼ c.	kalamata olives, pitted and chopped
2 tbsp.	fresh oregano, finely chopped		1 c.	tzatziki sauce
2 tbsp.	fresh mint, finely chopped		4	flatbreads, grilled
2	garlic cloves, finely chopped			

Method:

Combine ground beef, ground lamb, red wine, oregano, mint, garlic, salt, and pepper to taste in mixing bowl, using hands to mix thoroughly. To form burgers, place ½ pound of ground meat mixture into the bottom of the burger press. Push the long end of the press into the meat to form a well. Stuff the burger with 2 ounces crumbled feta, 1 tbsp. red onion, and 1 tbsp. kalamata olives. Place ¼ pound of ground meat mixture on top of the stuffing and use the press to seal. Repeat process for other three burgers. Cook over direct heat until thoroughly cooked. Serve burger on grilled flatbread garnished with tzatziki.

Yield: 4 stuffed burgers

BANGKOK BURGER

Get the same sharp and savory curry taste in your burger as you might find at a Bangkok open-air food market. Experience the freshness of cucumbers, onion, peppers, cilantro, and lime in this far-from-ordinary burger.

Ingredients:

2 c.	chopped cucumber, seeded	½ c.	sour cream
1 c.	chopped red onion (divided)	1 tsp.	peanut oil
		1	small green bell pepper, seeded and diced
½ c.	chopped Thai red chile pepper	3 lbs.	ground beef
½ c.	chopped cilantro	¾ c.	red curry paste (divided)
¼ c.	fresh lime juice	4	sesame seed buns
1 tsp.	honey		

Method:

Prepare the garnish for the burgers by combining cucumber, ½ c. chopped red onion, thai chile, cilantro, lime juice, honey, salt, and pepper to taste in a small bowl. Toss to combine and refrigerate until ready to use.

Prepare the dressing by combining sour cream and ¼ cup of red curry paste in a small bowl. Refrigerate until ready to use.

Heat a sauté pan over medium-high heat. Add peanut oil and sauté green pepper and remaining chopped red onion until onion is fragrant and translucent. Add ¼ cup of red curry paste and cook for another 3-4 minutes. Set aside to cool.

Combine ground beef and remaining curry paste in mixing bowl, using hands to mix thoroughly. To form burgers, place ½ pound of ground beef mixture into the bottom of the burger press. Push the long end of the press into the meat to form a well. Stuff the burger with ¼ cup pepper and onion mixture. Place ¼ pound of beef mixture on top of the stuffing and use the press to seal. Repeat process for other three burgers. Cook over direct heat until thoroughly cooked. Serve burger on sesame seed bun garnished with sour cream dressing and cucumber relish.

Yield: 4 stuffed burgers

THE BABYLON

Inspired by kufta, the legendary and exquisite meatball of the Middle East. Sumac is a savory purplish powder made from the dried berries from the sumac tree. No Middle Eastern grocery would be caught dead without it in stock, so if you have access to one, that's where to get it. They'll have lavash too; if they don't, pita works just as nicely.

Ingredients:

1	small eggplant	¼ c.	fresh cilantro, finely chopped
1	small red onion, chopped	½ c.	bulgur
1 tbsp.	olive oil	8 oz.	feta cheese, crumbled
1.5 lbs.	ground beef	½ c.	walnuts, chopped and toasted
1.5 lbs.	ground lamb		
½ c.	red onion, finely chopped	2 c.	chopped romaine lettuce
¼ c.	fresh parsley, finely chopped	2 tbsp.	sumac
		4 pieces	lavash

Method:

Prepare bulgur according to package directions and set aside.

Use a fork to poke several holes in the eggplant. Grill over direct heat until the eggplant is very charred and soft to the touch. Let cool for 15 minutes, then remove the skin from the eggplant and chop the rest. Set aside.

Heat a sauté pan over medium high heat. Add the olive oil and chopped red onion and cook until caramelized, stirring every 2-3 minutes. Set aside to cool.

Combine ground beef and lamb, finely chopped red onion, parsley, cilantro, salt and pepper in mixing bowl, using hands to mix thoroughly. To form burgers, place ½ pound of ground beef and lamb mixture into the bottom of the burger press. Push the long end of the press into the meat to form a well. Stuff the burger with 2 ounces of feta cheese, 2 tbsp. bulgur, 1 tbsp. eggplant, and ½ tbsp. caramelized onion. Place ¼ pound of beef and lamb mixture on top of the stuffing and use the press to seal. Repeat process for other three burgers. Cook over direct heat until thoroughly cooked. Serve burger on warm lavash garnished with chopped romaine, toasted walnuts, and sumac.

Yield: 4 stuffed burgers

THE BLACK FOREST

No, we're not talking cake here. Think about the kind of burger you'd want to eat after spending an afternoon hiking through the woods, foraging for mushrooms and this might be what comes to mind. Juicy beef wrapped around buttery mushrooms, gooey fontina cheese and marinated red peppers is a recipe for rewarding a forest-sized appetite. A nice stein of beer is almost not optional.

Ingredients:

2 c.	mushrooms, sliced		1 c.	roasted red peppers, sliced
2 tbsp.	olive oil		¼ c.	whole grain mustard
3 lbs.	ground beef		2 c.	arugula
8 oz.	fontina cheese, grated		4	poppy seed buns

Method:

Heat a sauté pan over medium heat. Add olive oil and sauté sliced mushrooms until golden brown. Season with salt and pepper to taste. Set aside to cool.

Combine ground beef, salt, and pepper to taste in mixing bowl, using hands to mix thoroughly. To form burgers, place ½ pound of ground beef mixture into the bottom of the burger press. Push the long end of the press into the meat to form a well. Stuff the burger with 2 ounces Fontina cheese, ¼ cup mushrooms, and 1 tbsp. roasted red pepper. Place ¼ pound of beef mixture on top of the stuffing and use the press to seal. Repeat process for other three burgers. Cook over direct heat until thoroughly cooked. Serve burger on poppy seed bun garnished with whole grain mustard, arugula, more roasted red peppers, and mushrooms, if desired.

Yield: 4 stuffed burgers